Forever His

Encouragement for Young Women

by Brooke Keith

Published by Warner Press Inc, Anderson, IN 46012
Warner Press and "WP" logo is a trademark of Warner Press Inc.

Copyright ©2013 by Brooke Keith
Cover Design © 2013 by Warner Press Inc

ISBN: 978-1-59317-702-7

Editor: Karen Rhodes
Cover by Curtis D. Corzine & Christian Elden
Design and layout: Curtis D. Corzine
Printed in the USA

The LORD your God has chosen
you out of all the peoples on the
face of the earth to be his people,
his treasured possession.

Deuteronomy 7:6 (NIV)

Dream Big

He who began a good work in you will carry it on to completion until the day of Christ Jesus.

Philippians 1:6 (NIV)

Did you know that God is in perfect tune with the dreams inside your heart? Each desire, each larger-than-life aspiration—God knows them all because He made each one. With you in mind, He hand-carved every dream you've ever dreamed.

While some of these dreams may seem unattainable, even though some of them may seem far too big for a small town girl…remember that God is a BIG God and His creations are no less grand. The works of His hands are a wonderful example of His own big dreams and His desire for you to have your own.

He could have stopped at shaping the earth. He could have, but He didn't. Instead, He dreamed up Saturn with its many rings and Mars with its mysterious storms. He made the wonders of the universe in hopes that billions of young children would dream of exploring them someday. He made

1

the moon's craters to appear as footprints in the sky. Perhaps that was what made Neil Armstrong dream of putting his own footprints there.

Everything in God's creation was made to explore, to inspire dreams and to stimulate our imaginations. The next time you find yourself saying your dreams are too big, just remember that your God is a BIG GOD…and He wouldn't have you dream in any other size.

True Beauty

*You are altogether beautiful, my darling;
there is no flaw in you.*

Song of Songs 4:7 (NIV)

Just this morning, you swept your concealer across the freckles that have graced your nose since the third grade. You scrubbed the blemish you feared would arrive on the day of your junior prom. Perhaps you even shook your head, giving a final look of disapproval to your least favorite attribute.

"If only," you thought, hitting the door, "if only I were _____, then I'd be truly beautiful."

If you have become the judge of your own beauty pageant, you deserve a much larger crown than you are giving yourself. True beauty beams from within. It echoes through the heart. It shines from the innermost corners of your being, making its way to the surface in a sheer masterpiece composed by none other than God Almighty Himself. Yes. You are truly a divine creation.

With loving care, God plucked the brightest stars from the heavens and gave them to you to wear

in your eyes. He wove together bits of sunlight and shimmering strands of moonbeams, then placed them atop your head, each ingredient brought from galaxies far, far away—just to be sure no other girl in the world had your same lovely locks. He molded each inch of you with loving care.

In the midst of your "if only" moments, stop searching your face for imperfections and seek out the perfect truth of a Father who thinks you're truly beautiful. In His eyes you'll find a new appreciation for every freckle. You'll remember the stressful week that brought on that break-out...and then, you'll remember that He brought you through it, held safely in His warm embrace. You'll gaze at your quirkiest feature and see it as the signature piece God created it to be.

An artist signs his name to nothing short of perfection. You are a masterpiece, a true beauty...a God-made original.

Only One

If a man owns a hundred sheep, and one of them wanders away, will he not leave the ninety-nine on the hills and go to look for the one that wandered off? And if he finds it, truly I tell you, he is happier about that one sheep than about the ninety-nine that did not wander off.

Matthew 18:12-13 (NIV)

You heard it in your kindergarten classroom when you were five. Your teacher asked, "What is three minus two?" And you raised your little hand, sweetly answering, "Only one." You heard it on the playground as your best friend begged you for "only one" of your Skittles®. You heard it on that date with the boy your sister warned you about as he pressured you for "only one" time.

Our society puts so little emphasis on the number **1** that we have begun to associate it's worth with negativity. We think *one* of something isn't worth much at all. Actually, this overlooked number holds so much more power than we give it credit.

If you were to read your Bible from cover-to-cover, you would find that God was trying to tell you the exact same thing. Did you know that the Bible uses the word **one** 2,295 times? In fact it beats out every other number mentioned in God's #1 best seller.

It took only *one* day to paint the heavens.

It took only *one* day to shape the moon.

It took only *one* God to do it.

It took Him only *one* day to mold the earth….

And it took His **only** Son to save it.

The next time you find yourself saying, "One person doesn't have the power to change things"… just look at the One who changed it all.

You *can* change the world. You *can* make a difference. You have a unique purpose, and you are the only *one* who can fulfill it.

Circumstances Don't Define You

So God created mankind in his own image, in the image of God he created them; male and female he created them.

Genesis 1:27 (NIV)

A tiny barn…

Tattered clothes…

A mom and dad with barely enough money to get by…

Jesus was born, like many of us—into the *ordinary*.

His home? Unremarkable.

His circumstances? Commonplace.

Ten fingers, ten toes and a belly button just like yours and mine.

While He was born into the ordinary, He came from the divine. He took an ordinary brown bag lunch and turned it into a feast for the masses. Well water became wine in His hands. Mud became a cure for blindness.

His outward appearance was ordinary, but what was within Him was extraordinary. Jesus knows that *ordinary* is a label for circumstances that only become reality when you believe they define the light within you.

You are molded in His image, created to be the *extraordinary* in the midst of the *unremarkable*.

When it comes to circumstances, remember…

You are defined by *Him*, not by them.

Give Your Gifts Away

*Each person is given something to do that shows who
God is: Everyone gets in on it, everyone benefits....
The variety is wonderful.... All these gifts have a
common origin, but are handed out one by one by the one
Spirit of God. He decides who gets what, and when.*

1 Corinthians 12:4-11 (*THE MESSAGE*)

Long before God created you, who you would
become was already on His mind.

Imagining your heartwarming smile, He opened
the door to His overflowing gift closet and began
searching through an endless supply of presents....
"Joann will be a great singer." He smiled, pulling
a microphone from the top shelf. "She'll have a
knack for listening to others too and a heart that
forgives without need of explanation."

One-by-one He pulled down each talent, each
unique quality of your personality and placed it
snuggly into one giant box. Wrapping them all
up into your favorite shade of pink, He gave an
approving nod and added a beautiful shimmering

ribbon with a handwritten note that read simply, "Love, God."

The gifts He wrapped up for you were not manufactured in any factory. They were not a mass-produced talent that He also gave Jill and Annie. They were made uniquely yours, sewn together with one-of-a-kind threads and patterns. They are a designer-original, so incredibly complex that no other gift in the world could pass as a cheap imitation.

What gifts did God give you?

Take the shimmery ribbon from your gift box today. Go ahead. Rip the paper…no one's looking….

If you have a song to sing, then sing it. If you have a story to write, start typing. If you have wisdom to share, speak it. God's gifts to you are your gift to the world, and He's counting on you to give them away.

You're Perfect Just the Way You Are

As for God, his way is perfect:
The Lord's word is flawless.

2 Samuel 22:31 (NIV)

You may not like your freckles or your lanky legs. You may not like your long nose or your chubby cheeks…but God does. He said so. "Before I formed thee in the belly I knew thee…I sanctified thee" (Jeremiah 1:5). Ponder those words for a moment…. He knew you before anyone else did.

Before there was a you, when you were but clay in His hands, He already knew you. He knew what He wanted you to look like. He knew who He wanted you to be. He gave great thought to the way your ears would stick out ever so slightly from your face. He closed His eyes and envisioned where each hair on your head would be placed, every line, every freckle.

As He molded your every unique feature, He gave you original qualities that are uniquely your own. He gave you gifts, dreams and talents unlike anything else the world has ever seen.

God doesn't have an assembly line. You were not a mass production of the same old tired parts and pieces. You are a God-original, made with new colors, new textures, new techniques. What you see in the mirror is a masterpiece signed by His hand. Honor Him by seeing yourself through His eyes.

From the hairs of your head to the very tips of your toes, you are perfect *just* the way you are.

Love Conquered All

I have told you these things, so that in Me you may have...
peace and confidence. In the world you have tribulation
and trials and distress and frustration;
but be of good cheer...! For I have overcome the world.

John 16:33 (AMP)

As our Savior took His last breath upon the cross, something miraculous happened. Every sin became guiltless. Every circumstance was changed. Every broken thing in your life was made whole.

As His blood flowed down each grain of the cross, love conquered all.

As you grow and change, your trials will also grow and change, but every battle you'll ever face has already been written down in God's history book. Each chapter, each last stand, every single "shot" fired...you've already been named the victor. The good fight has already been fought.

When life's armies come charging, you don't have to worry about the fire from their muskets. Nor do you have to run away with your white flag waving. *No weapon formed against you shall*

prosper, Isaiah 54:7 (NKJV). The victory has already been won. Grace fought the fight long ago.

When the battle rages in your life, don't surrender under the weight of your burdens… simply surrender the weight of your burdens to the cross.

Death covered sin.

Grace rose again.

Love conquered all.

He Will Always Send You Roses

I'll give her bouquets of roses.
I'll turn Heartbreak Valley into Acres of Hope.

Hosea 2:14 (*The Message*)

Have you ever had one of those days when you felt like nobody loved you? Days you weren't even sure if you loved yourself? Maybe you missed your homecoming dance because no one asked you to go. Maybe you missed out on your first kiss because the boy you thought only had eyes for you suddenly started dating your best friend.

When you're bummed because no one is giving you daisies, when you're down because nobody is sending you roses…just look around. God has planted millions of them just for you. He's adorned your backyard with dandelions so bright and yellow they always catch your eye. He's placed a wildflower on the sidewalk especially for you to wear in your hair. He's planted seeds yet to spring forth, just to be certain there will never be a day in your life without flowers.

When no one else seems to care, God does. He's so in love with you He doesn't just send you roses, He creates new breeds of them everyday just to keep things fresh. Even with the beauty and vast number of all the roses, He has yet to find one as beautiful as you are to Him.

Someday God will send you a husband who will bring you daffodils, just because…but don't think that will stop Him from sending you flowers. Whether they're growing in your backyard or are handed to you by a nervous boy on your doorstep, God's still the one who made them… with you in mind.

No matter how old you grow, no matter who steals your heart…there will never be a day He won't send you roses.

Kissing Frogs

*"Make it tomorrow." Moses said, "Tomorrow it is—
so you'll realize that there is no God like our God.
The frogs will be gone."*

Exodus 8:10 (*The Message*)

Once you begin dating, you may find yourself in some difficult situations. A simple kiss and hug good-night may start to turn into more. The boy you're dating may even try to persuade you to do things you are not comfortable with. He might try to win you over with sweet words, loving touches and promises for the future.

Of all the millions of males who have uttered sweet nothings and pretty phrases, most have one thing in common: They aren't looking for happily ever after. They're simply looking for a happy ending.

The devil's not ugly. In fact, he's charming and witty—a toad in disguise. Temptation may ride in on his trusty steed and sweep you off your feet. He might even gallop away with you into the sunset, his perfect locks blowing in the breeze…

but I assure you, that good looking so-and-so isn't headed for the castle.

We women are plagued with the diaper complex. "I can *change* him," we tell ourselves. "He can change." But the truth is, if a guy needs changing, it's not *your* job to do it.

Don't be fooled. You cannot turn a frog into a prince. Only God can do that. You have to trust that God has already written your fairy tale. He's the "author and the finisher" of your very own storybook ending. It's bound to be a *New York Times* best seller. He's woven His goodness into every page and He's signed His name to your copy.

When your father is a King, you don't have to go around kissing frogs. There are plenty of princes in the kingdom, and you don't have to settle for the ones croaking in the pond.

Love Begets Love

Whoever does not love does not know God,
because God is love.

1 John 4:8 (NIV)

We keep their secrets and swear not to tell a soul that they still sleep with their teddy bear, Mr. Fuzzy Butt. We lend them our favorite dress even though they accidentally shrunk our favorite sweater… twice. We create our own embarrassing diversions to turn the attention away from the toilet paper stuck to *their* shoe. Yes. The crazy things we do for our friends can be summed up in one four-letter word…*love.*

When it comes to love, there was never a woman who cared more for her friend than Ruth cared for Naomi. After she lost her husband and her sons, Naomi was going to return to her homeland of Bethlehem and live out her days alone. In her old age she didn't want to become a burden to her young friend and daughter-in-law, Ruth.

While it would have been more logical for Ruth to wave good-bye, and a lot less trouble to send

her a postcard via carrier pigeon, Ruth loved her friend Naomi so much she left behind all she knew, hopped on the back of a mule and followed Naomi all the way to Bethlehem. She loved her *that* much.

Once they got settled, Ruth went to the fields alone to gather the leftover wheat from another man's farm. One day he noticed her in the field and when he learned what she was doing, he told her to leave the leftovers…and take her pick of the crop.

Fortunately, the man was a relative of Naomi's and Ruth's. He thought she was so kind and so lovely he instantly became smitten with her. Not long after, the two were wed and they had a son. The great King David was one of their descendants.

Just like you, Ruth did some pretty crazy things for the love of her friends. She left the home she knew and loved, on the back of a mule no less. She worked in the fields alone. She ate leftover wheat for *weeks*. While Ruth did some pretty unconventional things, God made her living proof that love is *never* a common thing.

You can never love too much. You can never give it all away because you just keep making more. When you're following God's orders, you can never do anything too crazy for friendship.

Love begets love. All the love you give away comes back to you full circle. Like Naomi and Ruth—wherever there is love, there is God. And one act of love can set off the domino effect in your life.

Love everyone like nobody else in the world loves them…and God will put people in your life that love you like nobody else.

True Love Waits

And now these three remain: faith, hope and love.
But the greatest of these is love.

1 Corinthians 13:13 (NIV)

The world would like us to believe that love is a spontaneous romp on the beach, a sultry steamed-up affair, something ripped from the pages of a romance novel. Our society seems to think that an intimate, physical relationship is a normal part of loving someone—*anyone.*

But when it comes to true romance, the Bible's take on it is the only book that really counts. Why is it the be-all, end-all on relationships? Because not only did God create people, He created the love between them. Among the stars, the flowers, the trees, even the untold secrets yet to be discovered in our universe, God counts His greatest creation as love. He's the original Dr. Romance. He knows the subject. He created it.

In 1 Corinthians God describes love more perfectly than any TV special, more precisely than any novelist ever could. In true God-like fashion,

even as He wrote the words of that very Scripture verse, He thought of you. When He looked out across the universe, it wasn't the Milky Way that stole His attention—it was *you* and He wanted to make sure that you knew it.

The first words He wrote in love's description were a trio of beautiful wonder: "Love is patient." When you're faced with the ever-wandering thought of what love is, that's all you really need to know. True love is patient. It grows patiently. It *waits* patiently.

Love Abounds for You

I'm absolutely convinced that nothing—nothing living or dead, angelic or demonic, today or tomorrow, high or low, thinkable or unthinkable—absolutely nothing can get between us and God's love.

Romans 8:31 (*The Message*)

Wherever you go, you're totally surrounded by it at all times. Whatever you do, it encompasses you at all moments. It's God's love…and it abounds for you from sun up to sun down. No matter where you roam, it's always with you.

In moments of despair, His face is nearer than you can imagine. On cold, lonely days look closer; you'll see His breath on the wind. On a sunny afternoon, consider the sunlight on your shoulder…it's His warm embrace.

There is nowhere you can go from the promise of His grace. There's not *anything* you can do that will change the way He feels about you—not anything. Nothing you could think or say or even think about saying could keep Him away… He loves you that much.

He could be anywhere in the world, yet He chose to be right here with you. He could love anyone in the universe…yet He chooses to give you His adoration. He could have given His heart to any girl in the world…and He gave it to *you* to hold in the palm of your hand.

He Knows

*We don't have a priest who is out of touch with reality.
He's been through weakness and testing,
experienced it all—all but the sin.*

Hebrew 4:15 (*THE MESSAGE*)

If there was ever a man who understood the
burdens of this life it was Jesus.

He was tested and tried. Mocked and
persecuted. He knew what it felt like to stand before temptation. He knew the loneliness of feeling
like nobody else in the whole wide world understood. He knew the bittersweet sovereignty of His
purpose—to bear a cross no other man had the
power to carry.

Even as Jesus prepared to die, He didn't find
consolation in the comfort of His friends. He
didn't seek rest in the arms of His mother. Instead,
He snuck away into the solitude of the garden.
He went away to be with the only One who could
truly understand.

In your own young life you will brave many hills, just as Jesus once braved the hill of Calvary.

You will suffer your own persecutions and temptations. You will stand in the shadow of your own cross.

In these moments, you will not find yourself at the doorstep of a good friend. Nor will the comfort of a mother's love suffice. Sometime before the dawn, you too will find yourself kneeling down in the garden, talking with the One who already knows exactly what you're going through.

Whatever your circumstance, temptation, anger, pain or loss, and no matter the size or shape of your cross, if you'll turn around for but a moment, you'll find a helping hand.

Jesus will never let you carry your burdens alone…because nobody knows the weight of a cross like the one with scars on His hands.

Run, Joseph, Run

There hath no temptation taken you but such as is common to man: but God is faithful, who will not suffer you to be tempted above that ye are able; but will with the temptation also make a way to escape, that ye may be able to bear it.

1 Corinthians 10:13 (KJV)

You can hold your own. You can stand your ground...and then suddenly you're all alone. He looks so cute. He smells so good. He leans in to kiss you and suddenly...you're tempted. "No one feels like I do about this guy. Nobody knows how difficult it is to withstand temptation like this!"

Okay. Freeze frame right here—one word, *Joseph*. Joseph knew exactly what you're feeling right this very moment.

One starry evening, Potiphar's wife decided Joseph was about as cute as the middle Jonas brother. One look at him and she was making it pretty clear she wanted him, and she meant business.

Now, Joseph, being a human being, couldn't help but be tempted, but he didn't let his thoughts take flight—nope. While Potiphar's wife had provided the temptation, God had provided a door.

Literally.

Before you could say Nikes®, Adidas® and Converse®, Joseph was out of the door so fast he could have gotten millions to advertise sneakers during prime time.

In true God-like fashion, He had made a way out. He'd orchestrated every detail that Joseph needed to get out of Dodge…quickly.

While it may sound extreme, when temptation comes, you can't always pull away from it. Sometimes, you have to get out of Dodge. You've got to power walk, sprint, do the 100-yard-dash. You've got to do whatever you've got to do, to get away from that temptation quickly.

When the walls are closing in around you, take a second glance. You'll always find that in every tempting situation, God provides a door…or a very scalable window.

Peace in a Pod

Be sober, be vigilant; because your adversary the devil, as a roaring lion, walketh about, seeking whom he may devour.

1 Peter 5:8 (KJV)

Have you ever had a dog that only seemed interested in you when you had a plate of food at dinner? "Pet me! Pet me!" His tail would wag. Or maybe he would do the complete opposite and run off with one of your socks in hopes you would run after him, trying to catch him to give him a good scolding.

While Fido had a lot of tricks up his sleeve—er, paws—you knew ultimately that he wasn't really trying to play with you. He didn't really give a rip about your sock, nor did he want to get his tummy rubbed in that spot that made his leg kick.

No…all he really wanted was a chance at your peas.

The enemy is a lot like a sneaky little pooch. Even if he toys with them, he isn't really after your

relationship or your friendship. He's not after your grades or your job. No, when it boils right down to it, all he really wants is a chance at your peace.

Don't give him the satisfaction of distraction. When you choose to keep your joy in every situation, sooner or later, he'll just walk off with his tail between his legs. Serves him right...the devil isn't worth your peas anyhow.

Give Him Your Ear

Trust God from the bottom of your heart; don't try to figure out everything on your own. Listen for God's voice in everything you do, everywhere you go; he's the one who will keep you on track.

Proverbs 3:5 (*The Message*)

Walking away from temptation can be tough, can't it? It's so difficult when your curiosity says "yes" but your spirit says "no."

You don't want to be a prude. Sooner or later, what was once a logical conversation in your mind becomes less and less rational. "What could it hurt? I'm not sure I want to stop."

And then?

Just when the voices in your head become so loud you can barely hear yourself think anymore, somewhere, somehow, you hear Him. Sometimes it's a gentle, soft voice; sometimes it's simply in that conviction you just cannot shake.

In the midst of all those voices, His and yours, stop and give Him your ear…. He's got something very important to say.

He wants to tell you that while temptation has taken hold of your body, He has taken hold of your heart. He's holding on to it tightly…and He's not crying "uncle." He's not letting you go without a fight.

When you can't hear God calling, listen closer. He's that tiny voice far too often muffled by life. He's that voice of reason saying, "Slow down. I'll help you walk away."

He's Not a Quitter

I will never leave you nor forsake you.

Hebrews 13:5 (ESV)

Father, I AM, Alpha, Omega, Beginning and End. While God's been called many things, He's never been called a quitter. If you are facing an uphill battle in your life, it's important to know that He doesn't make His children quitters either.

While you may think you cannot keep going, and though you may feel like you cannot fight any longer, He knows better. He knows you are a strong, resilient, very capable someone. He knows so because He created you.

Before you ever saw the ascending hills that would grace the map of your life, long before you knew you'd find yourself scaling those rocky ledges— God knew. He knew you'd be braving this mountain so He equipped you with a safety cord and a tour guide who knows an uphill climb like the scars on the backs of His hands.

When trouble comes, keep on keeping on. When the elevation rises, keep looking up. You're not alone. He'll give you all that you need to make the climb, and He'll see to it that you make it to the top of the mountain, held safely in His arms.

Don't give up on yourself just yet. When you're going through the wringer, take a close look at your manufacturer's tag. You'll find that you were made to hold up to any wash cycle life throws your way.

Enough

But he said to me, "My grace is sufficient for you."

2 Corinthians 12:9 (NIV)

Whether you've been tormented by your past, by temptation or guilt, someone has been there before you. Paul was a guy who could certainly understand hardship. Tormented by visions, Paul went to God, pleading, "Help me out, God! You've got to take this burden away. It's too much to bear!"

God's reply came simply, yet wonderfully as He turned to Paul and said, "My grace is sufficient for you."

In *Webster's Dictionary* you will find the term *sufficient* means: *"enough to meet the needs of any situation."*

God told Paul that through trial and tribulation, His grace would be enough. Just as it was enough for Sarah as she bore her first child at ninety years old. Just as it was enough for Moses as he led God's

people through the desert, just as it was enough for Thomas who doubted, and enough for Daniel in the lions' den. In every valley, in every victory, God's grace proved to be enough.

The same goes for you today. No matter what your temptation or trial. No matter what you are going through. No matter where you are or where you are going—God's grace is enough.

That same grace that conquered giants—the same grace that scarred the hands of our Savior—is yours today. And that grace will always be enough.

For Such a Time as This

*For my thoughts are not your thoughts,
neither are your ways my ways.*

Isaiah 55: 8 (NIV)

Has God ever lead you to do something that required you to give up something dear to you?

If you are going through a time like this, Esther would have understood your inward debate perfectly. While she was a mighty queen, Esther had a secret that could have gotten her dethroned—possibly even killed. Beneath her crown, under her beautiful majestic robes, she was a Jew.

Now during this time, Esther's people were at risk of death, simply for being of Jewish descent. This put Esther in quite the predicament if she revealed her secret. There were only two possible outcomes for an act of bravery of this magnitude. She could either…

1. Set her secret free and save her people, *or*
2. Set her secret free and go down with the ship.

She almost didn't do either until her cousin,

Mordecai, came along and gave her the council she so desperately needed. Esther sighed, "A girl could lose her crown in such a time as this." Mordecai answered through a messenger, "Well, perhaps, Esther, God gave you the crown *for* such a time as this."

If it weren't for Mordecai, Esther would have let a wonderful opportunity slip by—the opportunity that miraculously saved her people, the opportunity of a lifetime to faithfully serve her God.

Perhaps God has come to you like He came to Esther. Maybe He's asked you to reach out to a person at school with no friends to her name. "But I'm finally hanging with the in-crowd," you say, or "I'll REALLY be considered a dweeb if I start eating lunch at that table."

Like Esther, you will find it hard to grasp, but it's in these moments that God wants you to stop thinking about what you might lose…what you've worked so hard for…and start considering that maybe, just maybe, this *is* what you've worked so hard for. Perhaps God has brought you right here to this moment for such a time as this.

Broken Things

All the broken and dislocated pieces of the universe—
people and things, animals and atoms—get properly fixed
and fit together in vibrant harmonies, all because of his
death, his blood that poured down from the cross.

Colossians 1:20 (*The Message*)

If you were to walk down Heaven's hallways, you'd find that God's art gallery doesn't consist of perfectly sculpted statuettes. It doesn't house canvases painted in Van Gogh-style perfection or vases of blown glass that took hours to create. No. Instead, you'd find beautiful mosaics, created from none other than broken things.

God isn't a wasteful God. He believes in the worth of all that He creates. While He may like an occasional painting, or enjoy a fine piece of pottery, He rejoices in the broken. He prides Himself in the fallen mirror that came back as a masterpiece.

Just look at the main characters of the Bible. David was an adulterer. Thomas was a doubter. Judas betrayed His friend for thirty pieces of silver. And yet, God adored the true stories of that Book

so much He never felt the need to write another or to rewrite the true stories within it. He rejoiced in the broken things of life, especially the broken-hearted. If you read closely you'll see that Jesus was most often around those who were broken and in need of Someone to help them.

If you've been shattered, don't be so quick to count yourself as thrift-store merchandise. God's going to come along and make you a true work of art. You're going to be so priceless that only He can afford you…and He's going to showcase you for the whole world to see.

God has a purpose for broken things…you just wait and see. Don't give up now. You're so close to becoming God's masterpiece.

Starting Anew

Blessed is the man who trusts me...the woman who sticks with God. They're like trees replanted in Eden, putting down roots near the rivers—Never a worry through the hottest of summers...Serene and calm through droughts, bearing fresh fruit every season.

Jeremiah 17:7 (*The Message*)

The Super Hero Rose is a brilliant variety of flower that graces the garden of oh so many green thumbs. At first glance there isn't anything that super about this bloom. It has its thorns just like every other rose. It withers beneath the touch of a winter snowflake and bends its leaves to the wisp of a spring storm.

What makes the Super Hero Rose truly extraordinary isn't an external quality—but in its intricate root system that lies just beneath the surface. Through snow and ice, wind and rain, no matter how many times the plant withers to the ground, it always returns bigger and better—all because of its amazing roots.

This natural phenomenon isn't the only thing God created with strong roots. No matter what comes your way in life, God promised to be with you. While you may lie dormant for a season, God is going to bring you back bigger and better than ever. Whether your storm was life-induced or self-induced, you have the ability to grow back stronger and better than ever before.

The next time you crunch through the snow of a white winter's day, turn your thoughts to what lies just beneath the surface. Growing just inches from your feet is a summer's bloom, awaiting its chance to spring anew.

With the thorns comes every rose…from the coal comes every diamond…and through it all God proves faithful.

All's Not Lost...
Even When It Is

I will forgive their wickedness,
and I will never again remember their sins.

Jeremiah 31:34 (NLT)

The title above isn't some nonsensical mantra whispered in the middle of yoga class. It's just a simple truth of your Heavenly Father. All's not lost, even when it is. Whether you've done many things you regret or simply stumbled along your path, with God our failures are never written in stone.

God doesn't own a permanent marker. You're not at risk of St. Paul running off with your permanent record and making an ugly mark on it. There are no paparazzi inside the pearly gates who will fly off and tell everyone what went down. Nope. God writes in pencil and He uses the eraser far more often than He does the point.

What you've done is in the past. God hasn't just tossed it into the Sea of Forgetfulness, He's placed a cinder block on it, and deep-sixed it so it will

44

never find its way to the surface. There's no need to ask forgiveness more than once because once it's said and done, our all-knowing, all-powerful God suddenly becomes more forgetful than your great grandma.

When your innocence is gone, remember, it's never too far gone. Every day is a new page. Every chapter in your life, a new story. You aren't defined by the things you've done. You aren't shamed for the past you've lived. The only person who can shame you is you. So don't do it. Refuse to wear that stigma. No matter what other people write in their history books, God wrote THE book and He says "All's not lost, even when it is."

God Was Here

And he said, "Here I am."
Genesis 46:2 (ESV)

In life, things don't always turn out the way we want them to. We may ask for red and get blue. We may pray for A...and get B. We may wish for miracles at our fingertips and find ourselves twiddling our thumbs. It is in these moments of the unanswered that many of us simply give up on God.

If you are going through your own moments of the unanswered, rest assured that the tribulations of unanswered prayers are not a new phenomenon. They go back to the days of Abraham and they fast-forward to the age of a young Thomas Edison.

Thomas Edison was a different child. His teachers thought he was mentally disabled and his erratic behavior made it difficult for him to make any friends. I imagine the young Tom must have prayed so many times for friends. He probably even

spent nights crying in his bed or crying inside as he watched other children laugh and play. Maybe he had times when he asked, "God, aren't you there?" And, perhaps the silence of his lonely childhood left him in constant speculation.

So when the world didn't offer friends for Tom, he would just invent them, as many other children do. From this world of imaginary friends, came a newfound love of creation, for dreaming up things from thin air. Tom dreamed and dreamed and dreamed until finally he imagined some of the things that helped shape our modern world—electricity, the phonograph and even motion pictures.

While his prayer for the love of other children may have seemed to go unanswered at the time, it did not go unnoticed. As Tom aged, his inventions went on to make him a hero among children… millions of them to be exact. He inspired them to dream, to create, to never tear down their walls of faith and to just be content to trust that somewhere along that wall the Lord was busy, scribbling "God Was Here."

God has a funny way of being in the middle of your life when you think He's flown the coop. He has a way of considering our suggestions and dreaming up something one million times bigger.

So, when you shoot for the stars and miss, simply keep moving, keep going, keep dreaming…. You might just find those aimless stars were pushed aside for your safe landing on the moon.

The Gift of Today

The steadfast love of the Lord never ceases; his mercies
never come to an end; they are new every morning.
Lamentations 3:22-23 (ESV)

While the remnants of yesterday's ribbons and
bows have fallen into the couch cushions, and the
gift of tomorrow is a promise not yet given, the
present of the present is a gift that God freely gives
us each new day.

As the first peek of sun chases away the moon,
the gift of today is yours for the taking—no matter what happened yesterday—no matter what you
said or what you did. Today is a bright new day, free
of the weight of the past.

The sun is like God's giant eraser. With one sweep
of His hand, the stars cease to sparkle, the clouds
are picked up by the rays of a golden ember and the
sky is set afire with the most brilliant hues of orange
and pink our eyes have ever seen.

Just as God changes the darkness to light
with a touch of His fingertips, so He removes

your sin. With each new hint of sunlight, your soul—blotched or splotched—is made to shine new again.

The morning sun is God's gift to you. Don't waste the present in the shadow of the past. Dance in the light of the sun. The whole world's your stage and God's smiling from the front row.

God's Painting a Rainbow

How many sins have been forgiven.

Luke 7:47 (NIV)

Amidst the lingering clouds of a past you just can't seem to forget, God's trying desperately to get your attention.

As you sit and listen to the far-off thunder, He's collecting a pale shade of pink from a morning daisy freshly bloomed in Heaven's meadow. While you wipe the drizzle from your freckled arms, He is dipping His brush along the surface of the clearest stream. As your eyes fix upon the lightning, fading into a purple horizon of rippled clouds, He's collecting the greenest clovers from beneath your feet and adding them to His already brilliant palette.

You pine away for His forgiveness of the sin already forgiven. You dwell on the guilt already found guiltless. As you focus your sight on the pangs of the past, God has set His focus on a bright new patch of sky.

Move your gaze from the darkness of a past that's cloud-covered. Turn your face to a bright new day that's Son-filled. While you've been busy watching the passing rain…God's been hard at work, painting a rainbow.

You're the Reason

Greater love has no one than this:
to lay down one's life for one's friends.

John 15:13 (NIV)

A crown of thorns upon our Savior's head, rusty nails piercing His hands and feet. As He hung His head on Calvary, thoughts of you echoed in His mind.

Just when the pain seemed too much to bear, He thought of your face—the way your eyes dance when you laugh and the way the sun brings out the freckles on your nose in the summertime. He thought about the day you first smiled, the day you lost your first tooth, the day you had your first kiss....

While it was your sins that brought Him to the cross, it was your smile that kept Him there. He could have called His angels. He could have come down so easily. He could have, but He didn't. Instead, He chose to endure the pain because the thought of never seeing that same smile in Heaven was a feeling far worse.

Everything Jesus did, He did for you. You were worth that much to Him. When He was on the cross...you were on His mind.

He Called You by Name

Do not fear, for I have redeemed you;
I have called you by name, you are mine.

Isaiah 43:1 (NASB)

Before the first beat of your heart, He called you by name. Before your features took shape, He touched your face. He filled your lips with your first words. Then, He laughed as you babbled in wide-eyed wonder.

His were the hands that held up your first bicycle as your parents let go with their own. His were the eyes that watched in pride as you took your first car for a spin around the block.

Before you walked, before you talked, before you came to know Him, He knew your every moment. From a first-born lamb to one lost from ninety-nine, He left the fold to find you. When you strayed, He climbed the mountain in search of you. When you wandered, He wandered until He found you.

He loved you before He saved you. He knew you before you knew it. He etched your name on the palms of His hands. Before you called Him Father...He called you by name.

His grace abounds to you.

His hope surrounds you.

He loved you before the day He found you.

Let God Out of Your Jar

You are the light of the world. A town built on a hill cannot be hidden. Neither do people light a lamp and put it under a bowl. Instead they put it on its stand, and it gives light to everyone in the house. In the same way, let your light shine before others, that they may see your good deeds and glorify your Father in heaven.

Matthew 5:14-16 (NIV)

Have you ever caught a summer firefly in the palm of your hand? Oh so carefully you place it in the confinement of a Mason jar, setting it in the corner of your bedroom. You wait for a fiery show of embers, only to find that what once was an incredible light show is now just a mediocre glimmer.

God is a lot like a firefly. When you confine Him within the limits of your own imagination, you don't allow Him to put on the magnificent light show He is capable of.

When you let God into your life, no matter where, He's going to shine, but if you trust Him

enough to let Him out of your jar…He's going to light up your life like the Fourth of July!

God shines best when given free reign. Although you cannot imagine a greater answer to your prayer, while you cannot see any happily-ever-after ending greater than the chapter you are in right now… God's grace is the kind that can turn the page to something so much more wondrous than you can fathom.

Let God out of your jar. When you take the lid off His sovereignty, He's going to rock your world.

I Am

*"I am the Alpha and the Omega," says the Lord God,
"who is, and who was, and who is to come, the Almighty."*
Revelation 1:8 (NIV)

It is so nice to know that we do not serve an *I am
sometimes God* or an *I will be when I feel like it God.*
We serve an *I Am God.* We serve an *I was and am
and always will be God.*

It is completely breathtaking to think that
tomorrow, God will still be God no matter what
happens. Tomorrow, God will still be faithful.
Tomorrow, God will still be merciful and gracious.
His love will never change. It doesn't fade with the
trends nor blow with the breeze. There will never be
a question that cannot be answered with His name.
There is no place you will ever come to, nor a day
that will ever be, when God will not be *I Am.*

I Am has endless meanings and endless
possibilities. When you find your mind running
wild with questions and fears, find contentment
in those two wonderful words—*I Am.*

The Palms of His Hands

See, I have engraved you on the palms of my hands.
Isaiah 49:16 (NIV)

You play a very special role in God's life. You're His daughter, His pride and joy, the apple of His eye. He wants to give you the very best.

He loved you so much that He etched your name into the palms of His hands. He's monogrammed His key chain with your initials. He's framed your most embarrassing infant moments on His living-room wall for all to see. As soon as someone walks into Heaven, He's bragging on you. "Isn't she lovely?" God smiles. "She's talented. She's funny. She won her fourth grade spelling bee." And He still has your medal on display…and yes, He makes everyone look at it.

The love of a father is very powerful. It can comfort you when you fall. It can make you laugh when you feel more like crying. A father's love will work a forty-hour job that he hates because it helps the one he loves. A father's love will drive a rusty old pickup truck so his princess can drive the sparkling

new Corvette. He will go without, happily, to see his child go with....

And that's just a father with limitations. There's nothing he *wouldn't* do.

Now, imagine the power of a Father with no limits. There's nothing He *couldn't* do. God wants to give you everything, and He's got everything to give.

He doesn't want you to settle for less, and with God, you never have to.

When you doubt His love for you...just look on the palms of His hands.

You're forever His.